"I"

NO IN THE WORLD

WORLD

Sukhapabjai

NO "I" IN THE WORLD
VARADHAMMA

National Library of Thailand Cataloging in Publication Data

Varadhamma.

   NO "I" IN THE WORLD. - - 2nd. ed. - - Bangkok :
Sukhapabjai Publishing, 2007.
   168 P.
   1. Buddhism - - Doctrines. I. Title.
294.312
ISBN 978-974-409-870-2

Second Published in 2007
Published by Sukhapabjai Publishing House of Tathata Publication Co., Ltd.
14/349-350 Moo 10 Rama II Rd., Chomthong Bangkok 10150 Thailand
Tel. 66-2415-2621 66-2415-6507 Fax. 66-2416-7744

Distributed by Book Time Co., Ltd. "**www.booktime.co.th**"
Tel. 66-2416-3294 Fax. 66-2867-0400 Mobile. 66-1855-7812
Email. editor@booktime.co.th

Preface

❀

The Five aggregates, which are Form, Sensation, Perception, Conception and Consciousness are regarded by people with a wrong view as "self" or "life", and who utter: This is mine, this is what I am, this is myself. But the Lord Buddha conversely stated: **"This is not mine, this is not what I am, this is not myself"**.

The ultimate realization of the Lord Buddha clearly reflected the *Anatta* (selflessness) and *Sunnata* (voidness) of the universe and beyond. It profoundly inspired me to write the book **No "I" in the World** and present it to the world.

No "I" in the World is not a collection of romantic fantasy blank verse, but it is my effort to express some views concerned with *Anatta* and *Sunnata* in their various aspects.

The first printing, in 1979, of **No "I" in the World** was the Thai version. Later, on July 28, 1998, some topics were selected to be translated into English and printed as a tribute in celebration of my 60th birthday by Sandra Mackinnon. and are included in this book. For the remainder, I will try to complete the English version for the next printing.

I would like to express my deep gratitude to Nina Weerapan, who devotedly helped me with the complete translation of **No "I" in the World**, and to two altruistic editors, Sandra Mackinnon and Gail Quillman, and finally to Venerable Sompoch Sripundh, who kindly typeset the manuscripts, without whom publication would not have been possible.

May all of them and all sentient beings realize the state of "selflessness" and live their lives peacefully and harmoniously.

V.W. Varadulo

Hinsdale, Illinois
January 20, 2001

Dedication

I am not an eloquent philosopher
I dare to present these verses
To reveal some truths.

Wishing to share views with learned ones,
This, like a garland, is weaved
By the flowers of words.
Worshipping the marvelous Noble Truths.

Illuminated become humans' minds,
Closing the way to woeful states,
Opening the door of heaven,
Realizing harmful is ignorance,
Beneficial is wisdom.

Nobody comes and goes on earth,
Just happiness and sadness on its surface,
Which are sometimes temporarily alleviated
By the voidness beneath.

When mindful awareness recovers wisdom,
At the moment of contact
All actions are conducted by "no self".
Surface and rock bottom beneath
Will be the same.

✲

To
My mother
&
Rose Indra

Contents

❄

NO "I" IN THE WORLD

1. Repaying the Universe

✳

All things in the universe
Offer 'qualities' and 'values'.
Knowing these 'qualities' and 'values',
And giving them back purely
And completely are the signs of
Beauty, righteousness and Wisdom.

Mother and father possess 'qualities'
Being the 'original cause',
Offering us love and being cherished,
Putting their hearts in us
Without feelings of hatred or revenge,
Feeling what we feel and sacrificing.

Their guidance and care,
Which are external cherishings,
Are regarded as 'values'.

Teachers have 'qualities'
Complete with Wisdom and compassion.
Their aspiration is for their disciple
To have integrity, moral shame and to survive.

Varadhamma

For teachings and instructions
And all external contributions,
We regard these as 'values'.

The Triple Gem has 'qualities':
Absolute purity, ultimate Wisdom
And universal compassion,
Having perpetual cleanliness, clarity
And serenity.

Offering guidance, inspiration
And training to all human beings,
These external contributions are 'values'.

'Qualities' are internal characteristics
With constant unchangeablility,
Never depending on causes and conditions.
'Qualities' are unconditional.

'Values' depend on consumption
For external benefits.
Having the characteristics of vicissitude,
Changeablility and disintegration.
Depending on causes and conditions,
'Values' are conditional.

All things in the universe
Possess 'qualities' and 'values'
Within themselves.

Varadhamma

Dhamma gives 'qualities' and 'values'
To all things in the universe
Purely and with complete absoluteness.
We return both 'qualities' and 'values'
To all things, so that we are called
A 'grateful' person:
One who completes their duty to the universe
Which gives us life.

'Paying back' means equivalent performance.
'Qualities' are inner virtues
Which should be Spiritually returned.
'Values' are external virtues
Which should be physically repaid.

But repaying the universe is beyond our abilities.
However, we realize that the universe
Is comprised of six elements:
Solidity, water, fire, air,
Emptiness and consciousness.
To repay the 'qualities' of the six elements,
Is to pay back the entire universe.

Solidity has the 'quality' of strength
And unshakeability, accepting all things.
Repaying the 'qualities' of solidity,
Directing ones mind to strength and unshakeability,
Enables us to bear all situations.

Coolness, cohesion, and maintaining
A level of equilibrium

Varadhamma

Are the qualities of water.
Repaying the 'qualities' of water,
Ones mind is directed toward coolness,
Tranquillity and peace.

Luminescence, heat and burning fuels
Are the 'qualities' of fire.
Repaying the 'qualities' of fire
One illumines the body and mind
With burning aspiration and effort
For the destruction of all unwholesome things.

Light and refreshing and constant movement
Are the 'qualities' of air.
Repaying the 'qualities' of air,
One eliminates all undesirable things
With consistent effort

In all elements, being devoid of time and space
Are the 'qualities' of emptiness.
Repaying the 'qualities' of emptiness
One directs the body and mind to serenity,
Free from hindrances.
Voidness, being the foundation of all emotions
Exists forever.

Realizing the true characteristics of nature
Are the 'qualities' of consciousness.
Repaying the 'qualities' of consciousness,
One directs the body and mind.
Developing intuitiveness

Varadhamma

With every wisdom contact
Results in no exposure to Spiritual suffering.

In conclusion:
Directing one's life by maintaining the mind
In the profound State of No-Suffering,
Free from defilements and realizing *Nibbana*;
This is the state of reciprocation of all elements,
Or repaying the 'qualities' of the entire universe,
Or returning to the 'qualities' of Dhamma.
One has the free will to attain
Here and now.

For association and communication within society,
Pertaining to the utilization of physical contributions
Which we call 'values' ,
We repay with complete external activities
And behaviors
For a particular case or situation,
With respect, humility, gentleness,
Moderation, mindfulness and vigilance,
Within appropriate time and space
In each level of the process.

It has been said
Dhamma is a 'qualities' and 'values' system.
This may be true,
But there are causes and effects
For completing the repayment of
'Qualities' and 'values';
Both 'qualities' and 'values' are interrelated.

Varadhamma

Someone at sometime during the practice
Of 'gratitude'
May place 'qualities' as the forerunner.
Someone at sometime for the same purpose
May place 'values' as the forerunner.

If one attaches or gives importance
To 'qualities' only,
It will turn into an opportunity for crudeness
And casualness to occur,
With self-indulgence,
Ignoring the completion of appropriate duties,
Merely alleging voidness, freedom, deliverance
And detachment,
In accordance with the deceptions of defilement.

If one attaches or gives importance
To 'values' only,
It will turn into an opportunity for clinging
To traditions, rituals, and social conventions,
Never leading to Spiritual liberation.

Performing in the Middle Path
Harmonious in both virtues
This is as the Lord Buddha teaches.

Having realized one's own benefits,
One brings to absolute completion these benefits
With supreme awareness and concentration.
Having realized one's benefits toward others,

Varadhamma

One completes these benefits
With supreme awareness and concentration.
Having realized the benefits of both,
One brings absolute completion of both
With supreme awareness and concentration.

Do work of all kinds with a mind that is void
At every moment.
Along the steps of life's evolution,
One reciprocates for 'qualities' and 'values'.

May all living beings
Remember and think toward the 'qualities'
And 'values' of all things
In the universe and beyond,
Perfecting all duties for prosperity, success
And beauty
For the remainder of one's human life.

✳

Varadhamma

2. The East & The West

✳

Primitive man:
Dwelling in caves, forests and mountains,
Living their lives similar to that of the beasts;
With gradual evolution,
Acquiring an appearance clearly unique.

Coming to the age of intuitive study:
Questioning the utmost goodness in human life.

Ascetics of the East learned to prevent suffering
From arising in the mind, body and speech,
In various actions and behaviors,
But for the same purpose:
The prevention of all suffering.

Philosophers of the West studied the evolution
Of the external universe,
Excluding man's internal sufferings,
Supplying their secular curiosity
With logical reasoning,
Concluding with endless material creations.

The East studied the internal world.
The West studied the external worlds.

Varadhamma

The results of Eastern studies
Gave rise to Lord Buddha.,
To the Enlightened Ones:
Those having gone beyond the worlds of suffering.

The results of Western studies
Gave rise to material scientists and engineers:
Those who went beyond the many worlds of material creations.

The unfortunate ones in the world
Attached to the materialized West;
Spiritual evolution was beyond their senses.
Notwithstanding, the Spiritual factor finally controls
All external behaviors and activities.

The West embraced material gain
For the attainment of happiness.
It is uncertain when material gain will be complete.
But, till that time,
How much suffering must they bear?

The East realized that Spiritual happiness
Can be realized instantly when the mind
Is void of defilement.
Then, when one searches for materials,
Those necessary to sustain the survival
Of the physical body,
No suffering will be experienced

The East studied from the internal to the external.

Varadhamma

The West studied from the external to the internal.
This is the way of life.

Perhaps one day, human beings will study
And search the material world
With peace of mind.
Or use the mind with peace for studying
And searching the material world.
From that time on,
The true meaning of humanity will be recalled.

Varadhamma

3. Original Cause

❄

When you want a lotus or its leaves,
Or anything concerning a lotus,
You must enter the water
And uproot the lotus plant.

When you want to win a battle,
Fighting tactics are implemented
In order to kill the enemy's leader.
This form of fighting is better than
Killing a low-ranking soldier.

When you want to win over someone,
Wisdom is used to conquer their mind,
Thus becoming the true conqueror.
Better to win in this way, than by lesser means
From which surrender is uncertain.

When the body is tense, tired, or anxious,
The Buddha teaches us to know its nature
And to calm that nature with long, slow, deep breaths.
The body will then experience peaceful relaxation.
It is better to practice in this one way
Than to practice in a myriad of lesser ways.

Varadhamma

When you wish to solve social problems,
The state of Spirituality must be realized first.
For when human beings have moral shame,
Loving kindness, compassion, equanimity,
Gratitude and contentment,
All problems are resolved.

Because external behavior
Stems from the inner Spirit,
It is unnecessary to find a single solution
For resolving external problems:
Those of regimes, politics, economics, sociology,
Education or public health.

When you wish to solve personal problems
You are taught to prevent the most
Important defilement from arising:
The feeling of an 'egoistic concept'.
Then, all problems can be solved completely.
This is the most profound solution, far surpassing
The resolution of external problems individually.

The right mindfulness and wisdom for
The realization of Truths
Is of the utmost importance
When solving problems.

Human beings, refrain from heedlessness!
Study, practice and realize for yourselves
The 'Original Cause' of all things.
For then, and only when this process is undertaken

Varadhamma

Can problems be uprooted at their true cause.
For if not, valuable time is wasted
And you will surely die
Before your myriad problems are resolved.

✻

Varadhamma

4. Materialists

✻

When asked, "What is a poor person?"
They answer, "One who has no money".
What about the existence of
'Poor thought' and 'poor knowledge'?
Why is this not mentioned?

When asked, "What is a beautiful person?"
They answer, "One whose physical appearance is beautiful".
What about the existence of one
Who has beautiful virtues?
Why is this never mentioned?

They teach, "One who experiences sensual thought
Has human nature which cannot be prevented".
What about the existence of 'renunciative thought'?
Why is this never taught?

They proclaim, "Because of competitiveness in society,
Selfishness is increasing".
Why not proclaim instead, "Because of increased selfishness,
Competitiveness in society arises"?

They contend that, "Because of economic depression,
One cannot maintain scrupulous moral behavior".
What they ought to say is, "If one maintains moral behavior,

Varadhamma

The economy will not decline".

They contend that, "If a country is not secure,
Then religion cannot survive".
But we defend that, "If one has no religion,
Then humanity cannot survive".
Thus, our homeland would have no meaning
And become a land of hell-beings.

They accuse that, "Cultures and customs associated
With religion are out-dated, failing to meet the
Progressive needs of this new generation
And must be relinquished".
But the spirits of our ancestors whisper,
"The new generation has little understanding
For the acceptance of a culture
Which overcomes defilement
In order to become a wise person".

They say, "We are born to wander in the cycle
Of birth and death, unable to cease all sufferings
In this one lifetime".
But, the Triple Gem has loving-kindness and
Compassion toward all living things,
Demonstrating that our mind dwells
More in the state of voidness and Nirvana
Than in suffering.
Why is this never mentioned?

Varadhamma

5. Where They Are

❄

When school is finished,
Young students walk home in a group.
Their minds are focused on playing
And snacks at home.

In the market, crowded with people,
Their minds set on buying
Bargain-priced items.

When students of the same class get together,
They look only for their closest friends.

When a young man and young woman fall in love,
They walk together hand in hand.
Their minds fall into sensual pleasure,
Dreaming of a beautiful future together.

When grandparents and grandchildren talk
With each other, the grandparents remember
The past, and share their past with the grandchildren.

When people who have started cultivating Spiritual
Knowledge walk, they walk in meditation solely.

Varadhamma

They meditate on their movements.

When Bodhisattvas[1]
Wander by themselves, their minds are filled
With generosity, compassion and
Loving kindness toward all living beings.

**But for the self-enlightened Buddhas,
Whatever state they may dwell in,
We do not have the ability to know it.**

---

[1] Buddha to be

Varadhamma

6. For What Do We Learn?

✳

The foolish search for diversity.
They look for differences in all things:
The differences in religious creeds,
The differences in residence and terrain,
The differences in knowledge,
The differences in all living beings in the world,
In the caste system, gender, status and so on.

What do the foolish gain from their search?
The conditions of separation, fault finding, conceit,
Arrogance and dualistic conditions of mind,
The knowledge of external forms of existence
And the trivial character differences among living beings.
It is futile for the peace of human beings.

When human beings seek the similarities
Of all things in the world:
The similarities in religious creeds,
The similarities in residence and terrain,
The similarities in knowledge,
The similarities in all living being in the world,
In the caste system, gender, status and so on,

Varadhamma

They then gain a Spirit of Oneness with all things.

Even though we know that living beings care for themselves,
This is not the highest knowledge.
Until we realize the Ultimate Truth of the similarities
And resemblances of all things:
That all living beings are friends in birth,
Old-age, decay and death,
We must endure grief, sorrow and lamentation
With all problems, day by day, month by month,
And year by year, until the time when Universal love
Occurs in the hearts of all living beings and every level
Of peace spontaneously appears.

**Human beings should not be deceived by the
Differences in all things nor by endless knowledge.
They should utilize all knowledge at least one time,
Maintaining peace and harmony in the world.**

Varadhamma

7. The Genuine Refuge

❊

**Passing time
In the world of human beings.**

High will be low;
Lowliness will be high.

Difficult will be easy;
Easy will be difficult.

Profound will be superficial;
Superficial will be profound.

Real will be fake;
Imitation will be real.

Kinship will be an enemy;
Enmity will be kinship.

Praise will become contempt;
Contempt will become praise.

Happiness will become sadness;
Sadness will become happiness.

Varadhamma

Wisdom will become ignorance;
Ignorance will become Wisdom.

Virtues will become materials;
Materials will become virtues.

But one realizing permanent *Nibbana*
Will be constant,
Preventing all undesirable things from arising.
Things are not limited by time and space
In this world and beyond.

Varadhamma

8. One Who Does Not Realize 'The World'

✳

Who says that human beings living in the world
Utilize the benefits of the world?

The world has land;
Human beings live on the land.
But do they truly know the characteristics of that land?
Land is strong and dense,
Unshakable, accepting all things;
Even the external qualities are unknown to them.
Do not expect, then, that they will know
The strength, density and unshakeability of
The mind that will accept all things
With Ultimate Wisdom.

The world has water;
Human beings depend on water.
But do they truly know the characteristics of that water?
Water is cold and cohesive, maintaining equilibrium,
Flowing from the highest to the lowest;
It is the dwelling place of gems,
But even the external qualities are unknown to them.
Do not expect, then, that they will know

Generosity, tranquility, calmness, serenity,
Compassion, equanimity, and Spiritual Peace.

The world has fire;
Human beings depend on fire.
But do they truly know the characteristics of that fire?
Fire is hot, burning all fuels,
Both the beautiful and the grotesque.
Moderate heat creates organic entities;
This power has great worth.
Combustion exists in every movement of the body.
But even the external qualities are unknown to them.
Do not expect, then, that they will know the Fire of Dhamma,
That which burns all evil and unsatisfactoriness.

The world has wind;
Human beings depend on wind.
But do they know the true characteristics of that wind
Even though they must use the wind for breath
At this moment and forever?
Breath makes the body suitable or unsuitable for life.
Wind blows continuously, bringing coolness
To alleviate the heat of the body.
Before they start their business
And before death comes to them
They should collect all possible resources
To exchange with temporary breath
But even the external qualities of wind are unknown to them.
Do not expect, then, that they will know 'the breath of life',
That which cherishes the life of the Spiritual.

Varadhamma

The world has prerequisites:
Food, clothing, shelter and medicine.
The world has various feelings,
From coarse to fine; turmoil to peace,
In combination with rapture and happiness,
Until the state of clearness, cleanness and calmness ,
Voidness and eternity is realized.But human beings do not use
all these materials,
Neither form nor abstract nor beyond
In its essence.
What is the reason, should I say?
They purchase or have concern with them
By craving or clinging;
Everything is for supplying the ego of human beings.
They consume their own 'defilement';
They then do not consume the true flavor
Of the whole thing which is hidden
Behind the material.
This is why they are always hungry

**When they can prevent craving
Or clinging from arising,
They will consume the whole thing deliciously
And will receive the benefit
Of one genuine birth.**

Varadhamma

9. Knowing Defilements

✳

**Things which cause people to suffer
Are the defilements of
Lust, Anger and Delusion.**

Lust[1] attracts all objects,
Both cause and effect,
Leading to violence within ourselves
And others.

Anger[2] detracts all objects,
Both cause and effect,
Leading to violence within ourselves
And others.

Delusion[3] leads to uncertainty,
Confusion, misconceptions
Or blindness toward all objects,
Both cause and effect,
Leading to violence within ourselves
And others.

Lust may seem difficult to prevent
From arising;

Varadhamma

Its origin is in our thoughts.
The possession of various mental objects
Uses our bodies to achieve desire.
It differs from anger,[4]
Which mainly depends on external objects.

Delusion[5] causes people to act
Without mindfulness and Wisdom.
The results possess neither
A good flavor, as with lust,
Nor a bad flavor, as with anger.
When the consequences are fully realized,
People will reject the commission of such acts.
Nevertheless, all acts of delusion
Cause violence, both within ourselves
And others.

At times, lust may arise,
Causing the body to tire.
The mind is distracted,
Spiritual suffering has arisen,
Thus self-inflicted pain arises
Under the guise of 'lust'.

At times, anger will arise,
Causing the body to tire.
The mind is distracted,
Spiritual suffering has arisen,
Self-inflicted pain arises here
Under the guise of 'anger'.

Varadhamma

At times, delusion arises,
Causing the body to tire.
The mind is distracted,
Spiritual suffering has arisen,
Self-inflicted pain arises now
Under the guise of 'delusion'.

People have no love for themselves,
For if they did, they would put an end
To the violence imposed on their
Physical, mental and Spiritual factors.

People love defilements:
Lust - Anger - Delusion
Giving complete unbridled reign to these evils,
Allowing them to influence and control
Every aspect of their lives.
When thinking of this, one feels ashamed.

❋

----

[1] or greed
[2] or hatred
[3] or ignorance
[4] or hatred
[5] or ignorance

Varadhamma

10. Worthless

✻

Diamonds and jewels are worthless to roosters,
Who require rice paddies.

Golden cages are worthless to birds,
Who require freedom.

Gems are worthless to monkeys,
Who require wild fruits.

Virginity is worthless to a prostitute,
Who requires money.

Wealth is worthless to persons
Who have insatiable greed.

Time is worthless to those
Who procrastinate.

Lessons of Life are worthless to those
Who derive happiness only from the flesh.

Golden urns are worthless to those
Who have no consciousness from physical death.

Varadhamma

The Noble Truths are worthless to those
Who are heedless, lack responsibility
And suffer Spiritual death.

❋

Varadhamma

11. Doing Simultaneously

✳

When a musician follows the music,
He helps himself
And also helps the rest of the band.

When a housewife pays attention to her home,
She helps herself
And also helps the members of her family.

When you are punctual for a meeting,
You help yourself
But you also help the other members as well.

When you obey the traffic laws,
You help yourself
And also help the other drivers and pedestrians.

When everyone keeps a tidy home,
They help themselves
But they also help the rest of the neighborhood.

When a girl behaves cautiously,
She helps herself
And also helps her parents.

Varadhamma

When citizens are self-sufficient,
They help themselves
And help their country as well.
When you protect and care for yourself,
You help yourself
And help to protect and care for others also.

**When you maintain your mind in its original state,
It is equivalent to helping
The entire world.**

❄

Varadhamma

12. Why is it That?

❉

**Taking food at home is more comfortable
Than at luxurious restaurants.**

Speaking alone at home with family or friends
Is more comfortable
Than speaking to the public.

Sweeping a floor by yourself is more comfortable
Than asking others to sweep.

Thinking by yourself is more comfortable
Than forcing others to have the same thoughts.

Controlling yourself is easier
Than controlling hundreds of others.

**But it is most peculiar when people say that
Preventing suffering from arising in the mind
Is more difficult
Than solving social problems.**

❉

Varadhamma

13. Unforbidden

❊

**Who can forbid the continuation
Of day and night?**

When the body needs excretion,
Who can forbid it?

No one can forbid another's thoughts.

No one can forbid the love
Of a mother for her child.

When one commits an unwholesome act,
No one can forbid the consequence.

No one can forbid the condition of *deva*
From one who has complete moral shame.

When one creates the right cause,
Who can forbid the right effect?

No one can forbid another
From the Spiritual practice for No-Suffering.

Varadhamma

No one can forbid *Nirvana* (*Nibbana*)
From one who experiences
The absence of egoism.

14. Right and Liberty

✳

**Stones have the right to injure
The bare foot of anyone who steps on them.**

Rose thorns have the right to pierce
The hand of one unaware
Who plucks a rose.

Flies have the right to land
On uncovered food.

Snakes, when they are startled,
Have the right to bite
One who approaches.

Thieves have the right to steal
The property of the careless rich.

The foolish have the right to offend
Others with their ignorance.

The wise have the right to forgive
And eliminate unwholesomeness at anytime.

Teachers have the right to instruct,

Varadhamma

Reprove and discipline their students.

Those who dedicate their lives for others,
Have the right to be taken care of by others.

**A perfected self-enlightened Buddha
Has the right over all things
In this universe and beyond.**

Varadhamma

15. No Requesting

✳

**When you ask for food,
It means your body is
Lacking nourishment.**

When you ask for medicine,
It means you are threatened by disease.

When you ask for welfare,
It means you are lacking the basic necessities.

When you ask for justice,
It means you have been victimized.

When you ask for fame,
It means you are obscure.

When you ask for friendship,
It means you are lonely.

When you ask for mutual understanding,
It means you are behaving ambiguously.

When you ask for life,

Varadhamma

It means you are dying.

When you ask for freedom,
It means your life is tied in fetters.

When you ask for nothing,
It means you are satisfied fully.
And have realized the 'Perfect Life'.

✻

Varadhamma

16. To Know One Is To Know All

❄

When we know clay,
We know everything which is made of clay.

When we know wood,
We know everything which is made of wood.

When we know gold,
We know everything which is made of gold.

When we know diamond,
We know everything which is made of diamond.

When we know desire and attachment,
We realize the true meaning of 'self'.

When we know the condition of suffering,
We know all conditional things.

When we know the state of 'no-suffering',
We know all unconditional things.

As a child very well knows
The quarter in the palm of his hand.

❄

Varadhamma

17. Requesting

✳

**He requests the true life,
Not only the way of it.**

He requests sincerity,
Not merely words or pretentious manners.

He requests true love,
Not only consoling actions and physical embracement.

He requests justice,
Not merely comforting or verbal appeasement.

He requests real peace,
Not only peace that results from blood.

To whom will he make these requests,
While knowing everyone possesses nothing?
It is like requesting freedom from prisoners,
Wealth from the poor,
Self-contentment from the greedy,
Or coolness from the heart of a hell-being.

One must turn to within oneself

Varadhamma

And direct oneself at every moment,
Preventing suffering from arising,
Performing right duty with every step of life.
Then one will gain everything
Without requesting.

✳

Varadhamma

18. Value and Demand

❈

Eat when you are hungry
And the food will be delicious.

Sleep when you are tired
And you will sleep deeply.

Talk when you have the opportunity
And your words will have meaning.

Give to those in need
And what you give will be valued.

Be punctual in your activities
And your appointments will have importance.

Answer wisely when a question is asked
And your knowledge will be useful.

Recover your mindfulness and wisdom
At the moment of contact or feeling,
And the Ultimate State of 'Peace' will result.

❈

Varadhamma

19. The Ugly Person

✻

When they are innocent babies,
The flesh is soft and smooth;
Every part of the body develops beautifully.

When they are adolescents,
The flesh is tight with a bashful glow;
Every part of the body becomes attractive.

When they are old,
The flesh becomes wrinkled;
Every part of the body withers
Although it still offers warmth to the children.

When they become sick,
The face appears haggard and worn;
All parts of the body are pathetic.

When they die,
The body will bloat,
Exuding an overpowering stench;
Every part of the body is repulsive.
Others can observe only from a distance.

Varadhamma

But when unwholesome acts are committed,
Lacking moral shame,
The face becomes ugly;
Every part of the body transforms,
Becoming a center of hellish evils.

The wise, having realized Truth,
Glowing with a radiance unsurpassed,
Diligently protecting the mind,
Shunning unwholesomeness,
Prevent the ugliness of evil from arising.

Varadhamma

20. Duty and Privilege

✳

'Duty' is something that must be performed.
'Privilege' is the result of completing one's duty.

How much duty one completes determines
The amount of privilege one obtains.
Duty is to be done by human beings.
Privileges are given by Dhamma.

It is impossible to request a privilege
Without performing the appropriate duty.
Do not request privileges from human beings;
They have no power to create them.
Whoever dares to give another privilege,
Both are committing a grave error.
They establish themselves as the
Enemy of Dhamma,
And Dhamma will justly punish them.

One may request tools for comfort
While performing a duty.
Human beings can honor this request,
But do not forget that all tools are
Ultimately the property of nature.

Varadhamma

For one to gain in excess,
Another must go without.
They who request solely for privileges
But never apply themselves,
Never perform their appropriate duty.
Thus, the genuine privilege is never obtained.

If one actively performs all duties,
Privileges will increase.
If one performs all duties completely,
Both physically and Spiritually,
One has no need to request privileges.
They will have privileges beyond
All things in the universe.

✳

Varadhamma

21. The Remnants

When the sour taste of tamarind passes,
It leaves a sweet taste on the tongue.

When the rain passes,
It leaves clear blue skies with freshness
For the plant life.

When a beggar passes away,
He leaves an old musical instrument
And a dirty bowl under the bridge.

When a beloved husband passes away,
He leaves a moment of lamentation
With his young wife.

When our trials move on,
They leave behind the lessons of life.

When affliction passes,
It leaves behind peace and harmony
For one who has meditation and Wisdom.

✳

Varadhamma

22. Who is the Creator?

❀

Who said, "God is the Creator"?
In reality, human beings are
The creators of all things.

The differences in materials, plant life
And various kinds of animals
Create the differences in external appearances
And the inner characteristics.

We dare to create the wealth and poverty
Among human beings,
Birth and death in life,
Heaven and hell-beings in both this world
And in others,
Highness and lowliness in the caste system,
Wisdom and ignorance in knowledge,
Satisfaction and hunger in the mind,
Eventually creating *Nibbana* for the destruction
Of heaven and hell, good and evil,
Wholesome and unwholesome, happiness
And suffering, once again.

See!
God never created anything.

❀

Varadhamma

23. Compassion

Nature did not create the green grass
Only for the green grass.
It created the green grass
To feed the animals.

Nature did not create the sky
Only for the sky.
It created the sky in which
The birds can fly.

Nature did not create the water
Only for the water.
It created the water as a dwelling
For the fish and tortoises.

Nature did not create man
Only for the sake of himself.
It created man as a helper
Of all things around him.

Varadhamma

24. Not Knowing Oneself

❊

One dreams to be the possessor
Of a hundred or thousand acres of land,
While one does not have even the land for standing upon.

One dreams of various diamonds, jewels,
And material adornments,
While one does not have
Even the bared body.

One dreams of the perfect future,
While there is no oneself
Even in the present.

One dreams of being world-famous,
While one does not have
Even the title of being human.

One requests power beyond the mass
Of humanity in the world,
While one does not have
Even the power beyond the breath.

One dreams of being wise
In every science and knowledge,

Varadhamma

**While one does not know
Even one's own mind right now,
Whether it is experiencing suffering or not.**

25. Law of Circulation

✡

The inter-universe is only one;
Nature evolves the whole thing.
Helping and benefiting each other;
These things are part of the body of the inter-universe.

Every part is dependent and related,
Eating, digesting, excreting, and so on.
They work together through the law of nature;
There is no part separated to be independent.
Nature has created green grass
To be the food for cattle,
Earth to be the food and
Dwelling for the earthworms,
Water to be the habitat of water animals,
Sky to be the flying place for birds,
Fire for cooking by humans,
Man and woman to help
And benefit each other
And to reproduce human beings,
Not for taking advantage
By the feeling of 'Egoism.'

Breasts are for the storage of nutriments for babies,
Not for the object of sensuality born of defilement,

Varadhamma

Thus preventing babies from consuming.
It is as if the mother assaults her baby
By stealing the property of the baby
Making it 'I' and 'mine'.
Nature then punishes human beings
By making turmoil and chaos among them.

We should look around us considerately;
We will see the whole of nature
Performing its duty.
Responsibile in helping and sharing together
In the states of being a part of nature,
Not feeling the concept of 'I' and 'mine'.

Having realized this truth of nature,
Stop the feeling of 'you' and 'me',
Letting ourselves be a part of nature.
It is conditioned by the other things
And conditions other things continually,
Being cause and effect infinitely.
In the entire universe
There is no meaning beyond this.

Varadhamma

26. Creating the Truth

**Hundreds of artists paint the truth
With aesthetics from all inspirations.**

Thousands of poets create the truth
With rhythm, stemming from
The bottom of the heart.

Ten thousand musicians play the truth
With harmonious melodies
From the profound soul.

One hundred thousand philosophers speak the truth
From the ultimate wisdom.

Hundreds of authors write the truth
With the divine languages.

Thousands of decorators decorate the truth
Beyond all humans' knowledge.

One hundred thousand military troops protect the truth
With their whole lives.

Varadhamma

One hundred thousand conservators ensure presence of the
truth
For millions of years.

All those kinds of truth
Will not equal, nor be beautiful,
Nor harmonious, nor immortal
As the truth of nature that:
'This is, this is;
This arising, this arises.
This is not, this is not;
This is not arising, this doesn't arise'.

Varadhamma

27. If the World Does Not Have Me

If this world lacks pollen,
There will be no sweet scent.

If this world lacks a full-moon,
There will be no brightness.

If this world lacks forests,
Shade can not appear.

If this world lacks gems,
There is no meaning of value.

If this world lacks sensitive feelings,
There is no comfort.

If this world lacks friendship,
Love cannot exist.

If this world lacks wise people,
It is as if the progress of the world stops.

If the Lord Buddha never appeared,
And if the world survived,
It would be blind and tormented.

If the world lacks "I" only
Every world will have no meaning.

Varadhamma

28. Helping Yourself

**People with good eyesight
Depend on lightening
And can see the path.**

Poor people survive by being vendors
And with diligence, tolerance and saving,
They can be rich.

For an ugly appearance people
Depend on effort and knowledge
To become heroes.

A woman who meditates continuously
With self contentment
Can become a wise person.

Pets depend on the love and gratitude
Of their owner
To receive good care.

Flowers depend on scent and colors
To spread pollen for reproduction.

**Noble persons depend on wisdom and effort
To practice
For realizing 'Nirvana'.**

Varadhamma

29. Nothing Replaced

When there is no rice,
We can eat fruits.

When there are no elegant garments,
We can cover our bodies with leaves.

When there is no mansion,
We can construct a hut for dwelling.

When there is no clock to tell time,
We can depend on the sun and moon
To tell day and night.

When there is a lack of music to entertain,
We can listen to the cries of cicadas.

When there is no best friend,
Parents are lasting true friends.

But when Dhamma is lost,
We cannot search for something
To replace it
For being in a state of genuine humanity.

Varadhamma

30. The Identical Condition

✿

**The cow, whether white or black,
The mother's milk is white.**

The cat, whatever color,
Can catch a mouse.

The flowers, whatever color or scent,
When placed in a vase for worship
Offer equal praise.

The mother, whether beautiful or unattractive,
Gives equal love to her children.

Whether a King, Brahman, merchant, or laborer,
They cry the same tears.

Whether wealthy or poor,
They breathe the same fresh air.

Whether tiger or dog,
They both must drink water.

Whether pleasant or unpleasant feelings,
They both darken the mind.

Whether attaining temporary or permanent Nirvana,

Varadhamma

The mind is influenced to the same state of
Clear, calm, and cool.

And whether conditioned or unconditioned,
They both stand on emptiness.

31. University of Life

When one observes the body
Realizing the body is tired, rocking and trembling,
One then breathes in and out deeply
To calm the body.

When one observes the mind
Realizing excitement, depression,
Fatigue or anxiety,
One then brings it to happiness
And then releasing it once again.

When one observes the emotions,
Realizes that tiredness, anxiety and impermanent,
Fade away and are extinguished finally,
One does not grab onto
Situations or conditions being 'I' and 'mine'
This is what one strives for.

✪

Varadhamma

32. Living in Society

✿

Speaking of:
"We learn in order to get along with society."
This is not accurate and the one who said
It has no responsibility;
We do not know whether or not
Society is wholesome or unwholesome.
If it is an wholesome society
How much we become tired and suffer
In order to get along with them,
For all societies are subjects to change.

On the other hand:
Something big has to start from something small.
It does not start out big and end up small.

Why don't they say:
"We learn for creating peaceful society"
If a friend invites your child to take drugs,
Then you feel you must allow them to do so.

In order to get along with society
But you much not allow this
Because society behave in the wrong way.
When society consists of diversity
Each person may have created a wrong to society.

Varadhamma

We must try to correct this.
Both yourself and society
Otherwise we are born to only one life,
What do we do for society
With our independent wisdom ?

Do not just say:
"We must get along with society"
Because human beings are social animals
Such a statement is motivated by defilement.
An ignorance of human beings
Results in torment and suffering of the many.

The words; "helping society"
Do not mean helping in externals only
As when others lack material comforts
But they mean:
Do not create disharmony,
But to maintain calmness,
Helping to be rid of desires and attachments.
In the individual mind
Every one helps take responsibility for oneself and others
According to the appropriate cause and effect.
Then we will live together in peace and harmony.

In reality, normality is not something we have to create.
The conditioned as well is the normality of peace.
It means helping in the way of
Not creating troubles and problems.

Do not say, "Helping to create good."

Varadhamma

Because goodness and peace
Do not need creation.
Craving is the creator of poverty.
One who has self-contentment
Never lacks or searches for material things,
But uses only what is necessary.
With a tranquil manner.
Not for supplying the lacking
with violence and suffering.
Helping to get rid of craving
Is the way of overcome lack
Both physically and spiritually.
It has to start from peacefulness,
Not from trouble and turmoil.

In order to start from peace
Every one has to maintain the mind
In the middle way.
That is the highest peacefulness
That we have presented to society.

Varadhamma

33. The Choice

✼

When it rains,
If you do not seek shelter,
You will get wet.

When getting sick or ill
If your health cannot be restored,
You will die.

Human beings who are troubles nowadays,
If they do not go insane,
They will stop being troubled.

Revolutionists,
If they fail,
They must be killed.

When young people fall in love,
If they are not broken-hearted,
They will be troubled with the family.

When you are determined with the utmost goodness,
If your blood and flesh do not diminish,
You most certainly reach that goal.

Varadhamma

In the birth of one life,
If you cannot struggle *Nirvana,*
You must wander in the cycle of suffering.

It is like the green frog swallowed by the snake:
If it does not struggle to be free,
It will absolutely die.

❁

Varadhamma

34. Action Separates Living Things

**The child who does not obey parents
Is not a true child.**

The parents who do not love and take care the child
Are not true parents.

The disciple who does not obey the teacher
Is not a true disciple.

The teacher who teaches without right knowledge
And does not give loving kindness to the disciple
Is not a true teacher.

The citizens who do not respect and obey the law of the
country
Are not the true citizens.

The employee who does not respect the employer
And does not put forth full effort
Is not a true employee.

The employer who has no fairness,
And compassion to the employee
Is not a true employer.

Varadhamma

Bhikkhus (ascetics) who do not practice in the Noble Path
Are not the true Bhikkhus.

The religious devotees who do not respect
And follow teacher's teachings
Are not the true devotees.

Human beings who become only materialists
Or Idealists
Are not the true human beings.

Varadhamma

35. Experience of Ego

✿

Some listen to the Dharma teachings,
And gain confidence in it,
Understanding the essence of religion:
Suffering and no Suffering.
But may still worry.

"We do not have enough experiences in the world,
And can not be compare to those who do,
We must first search for more experiences."

This understanding is incorrect.
It perpetuates the "I" concept.
One who wants to experience more
Is the one who creates the permanents "I."
They think that one who has more experience
Is better than one who does not.

Those who do possess more experience
Are reminded of the permanent "I" from their past.
It is not certain that who experience the most
Will have more detachment,
It may be even more difficult to detach,
Because these people accumulate attachment
Until it becomes habit.
Those less experienced may more easily detach,

Varadhamma

Both situations depend on causes and effects.

In reality, there is no individual person,
Who gains from and more experience;
There is no individual person.
Who does not realize any experience,
There exists just in this moment body and mind,
Which are not "self" of an individual person.

In a moment of contact,
Don't let ignorance mix the mind
To become ignorant contact,
And concocts the feeling of "I" and "mine",
This leads to Suffering.

Then will realize the truth of nature that:
There is not "I" in the past, future or present,
Just as there is no single person
Who possesses the most experience,
Nor one who does not posses any experience.
This moment is their whole life.
And the mind is now "Void."

❁

Varadhamma

36. No Gain Without Pain

❂

When we pull something toward us,
We lose our energy.

When we put a diamond ring on our finger,
It covers the fair complexion of the finger.

When our land is expanded,
The land of our neighbors will decrease.

When we throw a grain of rice on the path;
An ant will have food for that day.

When loving-kindness enters your mind,
Hatred will leave.

When the cycle of suffering occurs,
The *Nibbana* will disappear.

Do you see? When human beings sleep
The other animals come out looking for food.

*

Varadhamma

37. Caring for Others

❂

**Do not complain
When the sun shines brightly;
We feel hot like others.**

When darkness comes,
All creatures are surrounded by darkness.

When confronted with natural disasters,
All creatures experience the same chaos.

When using the animal for moderate task,
The animal will have sufficient strength.

When kneeling to offer,
The recipient will bow to take it.

When one shakes another's hand,
They will respond in return.

When a child cries loudly,
The mother will cry louder.

When we suffer,
Others suffer as well.

Varadhamma

When we lose,
Others lose the same.

When we free from suffering,
Other creatures also realize freedom.

**Do we still not realize,
The resemblance of all beings?**

Varadhamma

38. The Assault

Do not move the rock in the park.
Don't pick flowers by the path side.
Don't pollute water in the river.
Don't contaminate the air.

Don't cut down the trees for the construction worker's bench.
Don't throw hot water into the field of grasses.
Don't hit or kill mosquitoes.
Don't threaten the domestic animals.

Don't strike at and harm others.
Don't speak harshly and hurt others' feelings.
Don't fluctuate the neutral mind.

*

Varadhamma

39. No Sleep

❀

If you sleep with anger,
We call it sleeping with the hell being.

If you sleep with greed,
We call it sleeping with the hungry ghost.

If you sleep with ignorance,
We call it sleeping with the beast.

If you sleep with cowardliness,
We call it sleeping with demons.

If you sleep with sensual pleasure,
We call it sleeping with angels.

If you pay respect to your parents,
Thinking of their altruistic giving,
We call it sleeping with the big and warm blanket.

If you chant to the triple gem,
We call it sound sleeping without nightmares.

If you sleep with awareness,
Preventing defilements from arising,

Varadhamma

We call sleeping of a wise person.

If you sleep with voidness, without "self",
It is as if you do not sleep at all.
You are always alert,
Therefore, having life with perpetual relaxation.

❁

40. Not Getting Along

❀

When the pig challenged the lion to fight,
The lion unconditionally surrendered.[1]

When the devil has power,
The wise persons will hide themselves.

When the adolescents fall in sensual love,
Their parents are ignored.

When the state governors need only "power",
Morality of the people is neglected.

When people desire freedom of self-indulgence,
The freedom from self-control is unmentioned.

When defilement impedes the void mind,
The enlightened mind does not appear.

When the girl accuses her lover,
In their sexual behavior,
She doesn't experience the highest happiness.

It is true, the Buddha's words:
Nibbana **is the highest happiness,**
Does no one care about this?

---

[1]Dhammapada

Varadhamma

41. Song of Praise for Gods

❀

**Primitive age, men lived in caves and forests,
Worshipping devas and demons.**

If the sacred powers created happiness,
The people called it, "the creation of devas".

If the sacred powers created suffering,
The people called it, "the creation of demons."

In order to encourage the gods,
To bring them happiness,
They prayed and made offerings
With different songs and dances.

According to their belief,
In return, they hoped the gods would give them blessings.
Sometimes, there was happiness,
And other times turmoil.

Until the arising of the wise persons,
Who taught in different periods and places.
Seeing the people performing music and songs,
Displayed their blindness to the truth of nature.

Then, they told the people to "Sing in praise of the gods-

It can solve all problems."
Having heard that, in the later period,
People changed and praise the gods

They used the old songs that once praised,
The devas and demons,
And changed the words to gods,

But still had turbulence of body and mind,
They believed that, one who praised the gods,
Is the one who comes out and sings a song.

In reality, even though they sang the songs and danced,
Their mouths praising the gods in the church,
Their minds were anxious and tormented
With defilements and sufferings.

They were deceiving the gods,
The gods did not hear the gospels and praises
From those persons;
They were still the songs of praise,
For devas and demons...

But whoever has the mind,
free from defilement and suffering,
Not violent to oneself and others,
Realizing the state of mind with is,
Clear, clean, calm, and cool,
With the right behavior of body and mind,
Experiencing the ultimate wisdom,
At that moment they are singing

Varadhamma

The profound melodies,
Praising gods within.

The gods hear their praise,
And give them a perpetual blessing.
Human in every level, age, gender,
In every place, time and situation,

Whether rich or poor,
Ascetics or lay persons,
Down to the old, poor, sick woman,
Who is confined in the bed,
Are all able to praise the gods,
The gods exist forever.

We can access the gods,
At the moment our minds are
Clear, clean, calm and cool,
Which is the state of voidness.

The silence echoes over the universe,
The foolish people will have
No confidence, wisdom and effort.
They can not absorb these virtues,
Can not sing a song to praise the gods.

❂

Varadhamma

42. We Have Not Yet Died

✿

When we have a life together,
How much we love and respect each other!
We can express only with thought.
For the physical relationship
We cannot tie up each other,
Or live together all the time.

So that when the one passes away,
The other one thinks of them.
It is as if they both still lived their life together.
Either when living or passes away,
The flesh has little meaning
For the existence of their relationship.

When one person attains the 'voidness',
And then passes away,
The voidness still exists.
When we think about the voidness,
It's as if we are thinking about the person.

That is the meaning of real existence.
If we practice to attain voidness,
When we die the voidness still exists.
It means we both live together forever.

Varadhamma

If one dies with a defiled mind,
When we think of defilement,
It means we are thinking of them
And we also die of defilement.
It means that we live together
In that condition.

If one dies with enjoyment,
When we think of enjoyment,
It means we live together in enjoyment.

**The condition of clear, clean, calm and cool,
Is better than either defilement or enjoyment.
So with the existence of voidness,
We live together forever.**

✳

43. The Vices

*

In the universe in which we exist,
We cannot separate physical and spiritual
Or worldly and mental matters.
Because having spiritual knowledge
Helps the worldly life.

And spiritual knowledge exists
Because of men in the world
Who study and practice spiritual ways.
When ever twoness is separated,
It is the ruin of humanity.

When a casino is opened,
A vice zone, a place of sensual entertainment,
That is immoral:
Supporting the violence, killing and aggression.

Supporting the popularity of the ignorant luxury,
Seducing people to the endless association
With defilements,
Supporting unnecessary knowledge,
Inducing the people to walk in a circle of delusion,
Wasting their time and energy.

When asked, "Why have you done so?

Varadhamma

It is violence towards yourself and others."
The immediate answer is:
"This is the way of the world,
Your is the spiritual way.
The worldly way is for the world,
The spiritual way is for the spiritual.

The world is the world,
The spiritual is the spiritual.
Why do you accuse the worldly life?
Doesn't every one have their own right?
Yours is one type,
Ours is the other.
It is good for every one to know many differences."

But are not those human beings
Who follow this idea lost?
While they eat nutritious food,
They also consume poison.
Do they not really die?

You cannot say the food is one way
And the poison is another.
That has nothing to do with it.

The nutritious food does not enter
A specific part of the body,
And the poison does not enter another part.
They enter the whole body.

Then which is more harmful to life?

Varadhamma

It is violent to yourself and others
It is the downfall of the spirit.
We should not support it.

The Buddha addressed:
Better to avoid evils.
Do not commit unwholesome acts.
Vices lead to ruin.
Association with the evil
Brings you to affliction.
Association with wise
Brings you to real peace and harmony.

Therefore, you cannot separate
The mundane and supra-mundane,
We will live our lives according to the truth
Which leads to the complete purity of,
Both ourselves and the society of the entire world.

Varadhamma

44. No Missing Opportunity

Do not say, "Life is hopeless,
We missed the most important opportunity of a life time."
Because hopelessness and missing
The most important of opportunity of a lifetime
Are the problems of one, who desires
Material gain and doesn't possess it.

If they know that
The most important thing in human life
Is to attain "voidness",
Having a mind free from defilements,
Greed, anger and delusion.
We will not be hopeless,
Or miss any opportunity,
Because even now and forever
Our minds exist with "voidness".

"Voidness" is not a thing
That has gone and never returned,
For us to be hopeless
And miss opportunities,
But "voidness" is the foundation of all things,
Existed before any thing else,
And will last perpetually.

Varadhamma

It will be missed opportunity
For the heedless one
Who tries to create suffering
To impede "voidness".

The material value that has faded,
Even though it has worth and meaning,
Benefits us not more than the
"Feeling of happiness",
Which we can recreate here and now.

But, even the "Feeling of happiness"
Is the condition of impermanence and non-self:
It only shakes the mind temporarily,
Unlike the "Freedom from defilement",
Which is genuinely clean, clear and calm.

Knowing this truth,
We should be cautious and stop
The condition that arises
When contact occurs through the six sense organs.
Existing with the "voidness" or "emptiness",
There is hopefulness and good fortune forever.
Everyone has equal opportunity.

Varadhamma

45. Delight with Nature

❀

The law of nature evolved nature
Such as the sun, the moon, the sky,
The cotton-like clouds, the mountains,
The caves, the forests, the seas, the rivers
And so on.

With different qualities according to the law of nature,
Not for the beautiful art,
Or the ugly and horrid,
Not intricate or tangled,
Or simple and ordered,
Or not any oddity and misery,
Just for nature.

Human beings concern themselves
With various forms of nature
With different feelings.

Some see it as a beautiful thing,
Good visualization,
Good admiration and good fantasy.
They sometimes persuade their companions
To sightsee natural things in different places
For recreation or amusement.

Varadhamma

But the law of nature
Evolved nature for only nature,
Not for pleasant materials
To attract the human mind.
The law of nature, therefore,
Punishes human beings with feelings of
Boredom and disgust
When they view a place
For the second time.

Human beings do not realize
The harmfulness of their ignorance.
They search for beautiful nature in other places,
And again they experience endless
Boredom and disgust.

The law of nature evolved human beings
For survival with physical and spiritual factors,
Helping each other
In the world of all living beings.

When humans try to do the duties
That nature requires,
It is like a spiritual relaxation with every motion.
Unlike stressfully working and then
Expecting relaxation by viewing external nature
When weekends come.

When human beings trust relaxation
Or the cessation of suffering
By viewing attractive external nature,

Varadhamma

They are tempted to forget their practice
Of extinguishing suffering by wisdom
In their own mind,
So they do not encounter
The real peace in life.

The old woman who fixes
The torn fishing net
Is near the sea and maintains;
The scene is intricate and tangled—
The white rocks with many layers
Are close to the water fall.
With many steps,
The water flows down to the rocks
And splashes everywhere.

**She never thinks of this as a vision
Attractive enough
To persuade children and relatives
To come to admire it.
But she can survive her eighty years
With a clear, calm and cool mind.**

*

Varadhamma

46. Consequence

When clouds descend,
In a short time it will rain.

When hens lay eggs,
Their cries will follow.

When cats excrete,
The front feet will cover it with dirt.

When babies cry from hunger,
Mothers will lovingly offer their breasts.

When superiors lose during competition,
A rematch will follow.

When experiencing the true nature
Of all feelings with Ultimate Wisdom,
The realization of *Nibbāna* will follow.

Varadhamma

47. Not Only Being Lovable

✽

The modern scholars teach that;
"All persons desire to be lovable.
You must conform in order to
Be favored by others."
This is the teaching that brings
The loss of self confidence
Because of ignorance.

It is the teaching that is based upon "egoism",
Not for preventing "I" from arising.
Consequently, no problems can be solved.
We are unable to realize or comprehend
Which kinds of actions are considered favorable.

If the involved persons have defilements,
Should we try to conduct ourselves
In accordance with their desires?

That is the working of selfish instinct,
Not an inner study.
The lack of self-confidence
Causes suspicion and doubt
Of whether or not one is lovable.

Varadhamma

The expression of humility and gentleness
Is not for the elimination of egoism.
Giving and sacrificing
Are not for eradicating miserliness,
All for selfish advantage.

When you know you have committed
An unwholesome act,
You lack the responsibility to confess,
Thinking if others know of your mistake,
Their hatred and abhorrence will increase.

Creating the habit of flattery,
Lack of moral shame,
Doing good on the surface,
Enable you to commit unwholesome corrupt acts
For the survival of egoism,
Not having genuine loving-kindness.

Disregarding spiritual aspects
Because the spiritual factor is invisible
For love or for hatred.
Your living then wastes time,
Energy and expense,
Not achieving the real peace;
Everything is a temporary fantasy.

We should teach that
One should be a wise person,
Not having grief and anguish in his life.
One should not act violently to oneself and others

Varadhamma

With body, speech, and thought.
All right actions of body, speech and thought
Prevent desire, attachment and egoism,
Which are the cause of all sufferings from arising.

Realize the harmfulness
And the danger of misery in our mind
Every time we commit
An evil by defilement.
We have two duties to perform:
Preventing suffering from arising in every moment,
And performing our right duties in every step.
By doing so, we will gradually succeed
In preventing all sufferings.

The violation of ourselves and others
Will be dispelled.
Peace among human beings will then prevail.
Without doubt,
We will be loved by the wise persons
With Buddha as the leader.

Varadhamma

48. The Highest Perfection

*

Nirvana **is the state of coolness and voidness.**
But not monotonous and bland
And not complete emptiness
To the point where there is nothing.
Nirvana **is a combination**
Of everything in the universe
From form to formless and freedom.

This world is composed of six elements:
They are solid, water, fire, air, emptiness and consciousness.
Nirvana is also composed of these six elements.
When the six elements exist,
The cycle of life arises.
When the six elements do not arise
Nirvana appears in the same time and place.

Nirvana has the element of solid,
Such as density, stability and unshakability.
It is the foundation of all things.

Nirvana has the element of water,
Such as delight, cohesive maintaining coolness,
Without color, odor or taste.

Nirvana has the element of fire,

Varadhamma

Such as heat for burning the conditioned things,
Not allowing them to go beyond this point.

Nirvana has the element of wind,
Such as lightness, blowing away old age and death,
And doing so constantly.

Nirvana has the element of air,
Such as emptiness from form, time,
And the meaning of "all selves."

Nirvana has the element of consciousness,
Knowing everything,
But still feeling all emotions with ultimate wisdom.

By this meaning,
***Nirvana* is the highest perfection.**

Varadhamma

49. The True Love

✻

Do not continually be obsessed with love.
Do not request love
From parents and children,
Teachers and students,
Friends and acquaintances,
Husbands and wives,
Leaders and followers
Human beings and the universe.

We cannot feel or visualize
The condition of love.
When we cannot feel or visualize
The condition of love,
We grab onto pleasant feelings.

We have an obsession, a persist anxious request,
Insatiable greed,
Finding fault in people
Who deny love to others.
'Egoism' arises in those feelings
And leads to conflict and suffering.

One cannot achieve success by requesting love,
Whose qualities are coolness and serenity
From the burning heart of ordinary creatures

Varadhamma

Whose hearts are filled with egoism.

**One should emphasize the practice
By not allowing suffering to arise.
And perform the right duties in every moment.
We are then able to feel
And realize cause and effect
And will then have genuine love
On every level.
It is the profound right way
To solve all problems.**

Varadhamma

50. To Overcome the Devil!

*

The modern scholars theorize that
There is no "instinct".
Humans are born with purity
Not having instinct or evil.

Because of social stimulation:
"If they are stimulated by the right environment
Or avoid the wrong environment,
They will know for themselves
And gain the right intuition.
That is the enlightenment.
All problems are quenched."

"Do you see that, if there is a solution
It must be in the external environment
Or in avoiding complicated society.
Otherwise human beings must
Endure suffering until death."

"When you cannot avoid external environment
You must establish material gain.
So people get rid of poverty, not have illness,
And have higher education.
When a good example is given by society,

Varadhamma

Then the individual person
Will be rid of all problems.
The Dhamma or religion
Will have no meaning for them.
Practicing for the preventing of
Inner suffering has no effect."

Our knowledge is different.
We see that
Babies are born with purity,
Not having desire or attachment.
Later, when they grow up
They have feelings of desire, attachment,
And eventually suffering
From all causes and supporting factors
Such as stimulation and heredity.

They are not realizing deliverance
With both mental and spiritual power.
Still creating the feeling of good and evil
Which leads to suffering,
They know only craving or attachment:
That still is the "instinct" of the devil.

We must correct the devil instinct
By studying the true nature of mind.
Seeing that
We have neither good nor evil,
Nor suffering all the time.
Of course, the external stimulation still exists
And is unavoidable

Varadhamma

Because we are not alone in the world.
But when we contact it
With our six sense organs,
We can overcome feeling by the practice of
Awareness and ultimate wisdom.

Do not speak solely of external stimulation
But talk of our sense organs upon contact
With a person, with right or wrong knowledge.

The Buddha said:
At the convergence of eye and form
Arises eye consciousness.
This is called contact.
(The other sense organs function in the same way)
Upon contact arises feeling.
We should manage the whole thing
At the moment of feeling
By leading our thoughts, speech and bodily action
To the right way.

When criticized,
Loving kindness and compassion are presented.
Anger should never occur.
With enough experience,
Even though we physically live in society,
By performing our duties
With no inner suffering,
We can then destroy the evil instinct
With the right knowledge
That is intuitive wisdom.

Varadhamma

Can you see that we are able
To achieve enlightenment,
Ending suffering,
Even though we must live with
The devil person in society?
And when we all practice in this way
The evil stimulation will not be harmful.

This means that
The correct external stimulation
And our inner ignorance must be corrected
By being mindful and wise
Upon contact and feeling.

**Not allowing ignorance to arise.
With ultimate wisdom and awareness,
This is the right conduct
In every step of our lives.
All these things religion offers.**

Varadhamma

51. Looking Thoroughly

Do not speak of only morality,
Because it may create the concept of "I"
Being more morally strict
In comparison to others.

Do not speak of only concentration,
Because it may create the concept of "I"
Having more psychic power than others.

Do not speak of only wisdom,
Because it may create the concept of "I"
Having more cleverness and discernment than others.

Do not speak of only noble person,
Because it may create the concept of "I"
Having more realization of
The supreme knowledge than others.

But we will practice to comprehend
The condition of suffering
And practice to realize
The state of no-suffering
Because it is the opportunity
To prevent egoism from arising.

If "I" arises in morality,
"I" in concentration,

Varadhamma

"I" in wisdom,
"I" in the state of a noble person,
Anywhere, any time or any situation,
Then all "I"s will create the suffering
That must be avoided from a distance;
Then there will be no chance
To create "I" in all things.

Varadhamma

52. Do Not Separate

Having heard that
In religion we must eliminate craving or clinging,
The ignorant person will contend that
They must work to earn a living, that
If attention is paid to eliminate desire or clinging
Then no work can be done, that
Those who practice to eliminate
Craving or clinging
Are ascetics or those who are retired.

Most people separate those who eliminate craving
From those who work to earn a living.
If you do not work to earn a living,
How can you be alive?
But if you work with craving or attachment
Then you must endure much suffering.

If you don't have thoughts in performing your duty,
Desire does not have a source.
Not having desire or clinging
Creates enjoyment in work.
When not worrying about any things,
Work will be sufficient.

Varadhamma

Do not put those who eliminate desire or clinging
In one group and those who work
To earn a living in another.
Or those having craving or clinging
When they are young,
Getting rid of it when they are retired.
This is also incorrect.

**Everyone must prevent craving or clinging from arising
In any time, any situation.
When only the pure advancement and responsibilities
exist,
Life will realize voidness, serenity and peace.**

53. Right or Wrong

❄

Now is the age of material progression
But also the age of depression of the spirit,
So people ultimately cannot control
The materialistic exploitation.

Machinery will dominate the human being,
Life will become unmutable.
According to mathematics
The process of thought will be divided
Into right or wrong.
Society will create many laws
To compel the peoples' behavior
Toward right or wrong in their particular cases.
In the same sense, people will increase resistance to the laws.

Moral shame, loving kindness, compassion,
Generosity, and compromising will be dispelled;
Spiritual cause and effect will be forgotten.
People will wonder if this behavior is right or wrong.

When there is no law to dictate,
The people will use indulgence as a measurement.
What they are satisfied with according to their desire
Is what is right to them.

Varadhamma

What one is dissatisfied with according to their desire
Is what is wrong to them.
Whether or not the result will be violence
Toward their spirit and the spirit of others,
They are unaware.
Feeling will be in one extreme or another.
What one is dissatisfied with will cause
Feelings of anger, stress and aggressiveness.
What one is satisfied with will bring
Extreme delight, clinging or feelings of happiness.

For their own satisfaction
Even though they know the condition and appropriateness
Necessary for a person, situation or particular case,
They overlook those truths and conditions.

People will be unaware of self-knowledge
But search for the faults of others
In order to prevent themselves
From committing the evil
That is motivated by defilements
Both unintentionally and intentionally.

The youth will be confused about
How to lead their lives.
Questions will be asked,
"What is wrong with that?"
"Why can this or that person do it?"
And "Why can't I do it?"
"Is there justice in society?" and so on.

Varadhamma

When we say that
Consuming alcohol is bad behavior,
They will hate those who drink.
When they hear that
Having many mistresses is bad behavior,
They will hate those who have many mistresses.
When they hear that
Extravagance is bad behavior,
They will hate those who are extravagant.
Having heard that
"Waking up late is not good behavior"
But their parents awaken late some day
Because they work hard and are tired,
They will find fault in their parents,
Insisting that they are good for compelling others
But cannot do as they say.

The knowledge that depends on right or wrong
Is purely the knowledge of material things.
It is not comparable to the mind
Or to spiritual realization
Which deal with peace and harmony.

For the use of training,
In all nature there is no right or wrong.
Right or wrong is an assumption
Of the people who live in this society
Who are not very educated.

The ultimate truth of nature is that
There is no one who is right or wrong.

Varadhamma

There is only the result of the action:
Was there violence to yourself and others or not?

If there are violent results,
We will avoid those actions.
Everyone who has self-responsibility
Shun finding fault in others.
To solve problems of spiritual pain,
Teaching right or wrong by physical means
Absolutely impedes the real way
For learning the truth of nature.

The Lord Buddha has absolute enlightenment.
He realized the truth of nature
For the end of suffering.
Buddha didn't proclaim right or wrong
By the reasoning of only material things,
But referred to suffering and no suffering,
The actions of the body, mind and spirit,
Whether they are violent to yourself and others.
Using this way of reasoning
We know if we should or should not
Perform those actions.

In the relative level,
Human beings are different and not equal
Because of conditions of ability, status, time and space,
Both material and spiritual.

In the ultimate level,
The totality is not the individual person, self or age,

Varadhamma

Only the difference of cause and effect.
Some behaviors are different
But become equal by Dhamma practice,
Whether the actions are violent or non-violent.

Human beings are superior creatures.
Having the virtue of "humanity"
That does not exist in other creatures.

In a human mind,
Exist the moral shame, gratitude,
Loving kindness, compassion, equanimity,
Having respect and worshiping the worthy ones.

In society,
There is the low and high person
With birth, age, and individual qualities.
We must accept the different conditions
In the nature of each person;
Then there will be human society.

**If we live our lives in the material level
Talking of only right or wrong,
It will be a material society
Which has no spiritual value.
That is not the way of human beings
Possessing both physical and spiritual value.**

Varadhamma

54. The Justice

✪

There is no goodness in the human being.
There is no justice in the human's life.
Goodness and justice belong to nature.
What one creates is what one obtains;
This is the law of nature.

When one requests justice from a human being
One will receive a moment of comfort.
In a short time, one will request justice again.
How much one accepts the condition
According to that situation
Is how much justice one obtains.

You cannot expect justice from the judge, ruler, boss,
Or even from your parents.
But the justice you get
Depends on how much you give
Towards satisfying compromises.

The thought of detachment will quench all problems.
We only request justice
When we are the losers,
But never give it back
When we gain excessively,
So there is no justice in our world.

Varadhamma

55. The Original Problems

*

Because of being born in the world,
The world has meaning.
But you are really born in the world
If you have no eyes or are blind from birth.
Then you cannot see either pleasant
Or unpleasant forms.

If you are deaf, you cannot hear.
If you do not have a nose, you cannot know smell.
If you have no tongue, taste has no meaning.
If your body lacks a part,
You cannot know the contact of that part.
Most importantly, if your mind is absent,
Then you cannot experience feelings.
You experience the external world
Which consists of form, sound, smell,
Taste, tangible and mental objects
With your eyes, ears, nose, tongue, body and mind.

Eyes, ears, nose, tongue, body and mind
Perform their duties when they have contact
With external objects.
If one of the senses does not perform its duties,
Then that sense has no meaning;

Varadhamma

It is as if there is no sense.

In a human being, the highest creature,
When eyes, ears, nose, tongue, body and mind
Have contact with form, sound, smell, taste,
And tangible and mental objects,
The sense is conveyed to inner knowledge for consideration.

Don't talk about external objects only.
You should talk through the following three:
Sense organs, sense objects and knowledge,
Of the rightness or falseness of the reality of that contact.

The Lord Buddha says;
Being dependent on eyes and form, eye-consciousness arises.
The convergence of the three factors equals contact.
Upon contact everything will have a meaning.
Eyes, form and eye-consciousness
Are only one thing called "contact".
(The rest of the five sense organs
Function in the same manner.)

We realize that eyes, ears, nose, tongue, body and mind,
Form, sound, smell, taste, tangible and mental objects
Are not more important than the knowledge
Which arises with each contact.

Knowledge is not equal in each individual.
Some people know some things;
Other people know different things.
We cannot immoderately stand up for our view

That form, sound, smell, taste, tangible and mental objects
Are pleasant or unpleasant;
That depends on the condition
Of the knowledge of each person.

Speaking solely of material things:
Having seen a flower,
We say 'the flower is red,
But the colorblind may see it as gray.
Or we may say "the rose has a wonderful scent",
But another may say it has a foul smell.
We therefore should not assert;
We should say it depends on cause and supporting factors.

Judging quality and value,
We say that jewelry is the most precious object.
But for the rooster or ascetic,
How valuable is jewelry?
It has value only for one who desires it.
We then should not assert;
We should say it depends on cause and supporting factors.

We say sensuality causes temptation,
But for infants or one who aspires to *Nibbana,*
How valuable is sensuality?
It only has value for one who desires it.
We therefore should not assert;
We should say it depends on cause and supporting factors.

In the practice of no-suffering in a materialistic society,
However it may be, when we have contact with society,

Varadhamma

We have right understanding.
Realizing "the way it is" or the "thusness"
Of different phenomena,
We have no desire or attachment.
With right understanding suffering cannot occur.

We cannot definitely say
What the world is or what caused it to be.
The material makeup, quality or value of objects
Are not the cause of suffering,
Because people are concerned with the "world"
Under different conditions
Such as material, space, time and other situations;
Under physical, mental, opinions, knowledge,
And so on.

One who realizes the ultimate truth
Would not have doubt in all phenomena
And insult others because of different behavior,
But try to prevent ignorance or attachment from arising
And perform the right duty in every step of a process.
Then human beings will be equal
Even when external conditions are different.

*

Varadhamma

56. No Expectation

*

"My love, we see eye to eye.
Mutual understanding gives happiness."
(Sometimes mutual understanding
Enslaves us to love.
It creates uncertainty, torment and anxiety.)

"Ancestors had to work to further understand
The new generation."
(Why do we force others to understand us?
Are we too weak?)
"The depth of the human mind
Is very difficult to measure."
(Why must we waste time measuring other minds?)

"In doing every kind of work,
Encouragement is most important.
I like people who speak positively"
(Who will waste time for encouragement
Or giving positive words to anyone?)

"Oh! The domestic servant whom I have really nourished
Still has the audacity to steal from me.
No one can be trusted"
(Who can trust those who have defilements?)

Varadhamma

May all of you start to practice
By freeing your mind from suffering
And perform your right duty in every step.
And then you will obtain sympathy,
Understanding, and knowledge of each other,
Encouragement and trust,
Without forcing and begging.

Varadhamma

57. Something Should Be Praised

✳

They said "One gains energy
By eating bread."
One then is grateful to bread.
But in reality, the Dhamma which is within oneself
While eating bread, brings energy.
One who eats foods other than bread
Also gains energy
Only if one practices in accordance with
The law of nature, which leads to energy.

They say:
"One gains pleasure from visiting a big city."
One is then grateful for the prosperity of the city.
But in reality, the Dhamma, which is within their mind
While visiting the big city
Brings them the pleasure.
One who does not visit a big city can also gain pleasure
Only if one practices in accordance with
The law of nature, which leads to pleasure.

When married the bride says that
Because she marries the man she loves,
Her life will then have happiness.
She becomes sensually attached to

Varadhamma

The man she loves.
But in reality, the Dhamma which is within her mind
As she marries the man she loves
Brings her happiness.
A woman who does not marry the man she loves
Can still have happiness
Only if she acts in accordance with
The law of nature, which leads to happiness.

Some people say that
Because they have a teacher to instruct them,
They can achieve enlightenment.
They then respect their teacher.
But in reality the Dhamma which is within their minds
While they are instructed by their teacher
Brings them the realization of enlightenment.
One who is not instructed by that teacher
Can still realize enlightenment
Only if one practices in accordance with
The law of nature, which leads to that state.

Some people say that
Because one enters a quiet and isolated place,
One's mind becomes calm.
One then praises that place.
But in reality, the Dhamma which is
Within their minds when they enter
The quiet and isolated place
Brings them the calmness of mind.
One who does not enter that place
Can still obtain the calmness of mind

Varadhamma

Only if one practices in accordance with
The law of nature, which leads to that calmness.

Some people say that
Because one practices a certain form of meditation
It brings them concentration
And extinguishes all defilements.
One then praises that form of meditation.
But in reality the Dhamma which is
Within their minds while practicing
Brings them concentration
And extinguishes all defilements.
One who does not practice that form of meditation
Can still cease all defilements
Only if one practices in accordance with
The law of nature, which leads to
The cessation of all defilements.

Because people never realize the truth,
They must aimlessly wander,
Searching for merit, happiness.
They attach to the goodness from materials, time,
Space, persons and various forms of pleasure.
Eventually, they experience suffering
When those things convey impermanence.

**In reality, we must praise and respect
The Dhamma
Which exists in every place at all times.
Anyone who wants to be in any states
Should choose to practice**

Varadhamma

In accordance with the law of nature
Which leads to those states.

Varadhamma

58. Do Not Act Corruptly

❄

If you want to look, look,
But do not glance sideways.

Be prepared for appointments completely,
But never be impatient .

Be simple,
But maintain mindfulness.

Think,
But do not be obsessed.

Pay attention to success,
But never set expectations.

Tell the truth,
But never boast.

Unite to help others,
But never conspire.

Take care of,
But never long for.
Repair or maintain,
But never regret.

Varadhamma

Use Wisdom and effort to the fullest,
But never attach "I" to gain or loss.

Varadhamma

59. Un-Affirmative

✦

In this world there are differences in human beings;
Their strengths, faculties, views,
Wisdom, abilities, efforts and so on.
But everyone needs only one thing:
The state of "no suffering".

Their ways to attain the states are different
But the destination is the same.
The genuine Dhamma teacher,
Being the one who is problem-free,
Must begin with each person's problems.

Their different strengths, faculties,
Views, wisdom, abilities and so on,
Leading to the result of detachment.
The method of teaching and practicing is to progress
According to the cause and supporting factors;
Each problem and solution is suitable.
They must instruct and practice that truth.

They must not only assert the truths of
External teaching and practice;
There is no constant method, form or rule.

Sometimes Dhamma teachers have individual views
Believing that they are right.

Varadhamma

They then constantly assert
Their method, form or rule,
Regardless of morality, concentration or wisdom.

One who aspires to practice Dhamma
Is the person who consents to the
One way of teaching and practice of a master,
So the practitioner surrenders, and
Becomes a disciple.

Some abandon their appropriate truth,
Solving their problems
By following and practicing
The view, method, form and rules of
Their Dhamma teachers.
Thus having a new attachment,
The enlightenment or result of the practice
Of those disciples
Is to have the same view, form, method and rules
As their teachers.

**Those Dhamma teachers are only
Religious missionaries for their own
Particular opinionated truth, wealth,
Honor, fame, followers, morality,
Concentration and wisdom.
That is not the real truth for
Solving problems for achieving
The state of no-suffering.**

❁

Varadhamma

60. Do Before Get

✿

Do not say it is heavy,
Because that does not make it lighter.

Do not say it is far,
Because that does not make it closer.

Do not say you are exhausted,
Because that does not make you more energetic.

Do not say it is hot,
Because that does not make it cooler.

Do not say you are hungry,
Because fullness does not replace it.

Do not say you are poor,
Because that does not make your richness increase.

Do not say it is noisy,
Because that does not make it more silent.

My child, why do you complain?
All my life I never bewailed

Varadhamma

**But I did every thing
And I then had every thing.**

Varadhamma

61. We Have-Had-Been It

We have a duty to life both physical and spiritual;
Physical life ends when we pass away.
Spiritual life ends when suffering is quenched.
Spiritual life could be perfected here and now,
But the physical life is not complete:

The elegant adornments--we have worn them.
The delicious food--we have taken it.
The luxurious shelters--we have dwelled in them.
Fame and honor--we have experienced them.
All entertainments--we have enjoyed them.
All kinds of duty--we have performed them.
Illness and sickness--we have been through them.
Words that should have been spoken--we have spoken them.

Thoughts which should have been thought--
we have thought them.
Things that should have been loved--we have loved them.
Things that should have been hated--we have hated them.
Things that should have been confused--
We have confused them.

Only one thing is left
When we have not been,

Varadhamma

We have not had,
We have not known,
It has not passed through our lives:
That is "Death".

When it arrives, then we achieve our aspirations.
It is the relaxation, when
Work and activities are given up.
It is an important change and great victory
Which will never occur again.
It is the perfection of one human life.

Many human beings have already passed away
In the stream of their journey
Searching for the state of humanity.
One should look to the God of Death (Grim Reaper)
He is a real, loyal, friend.
Thinking of death is not a bad omen,
But it is the highest rapture and delight.

So one day in the future
We probably will have the opportunity to say:
Even death I have experienced.

✳

Varadhamma

62. A Good Opportunity

*

When someone steals your belongings,
It is a good opportunity for you
To be giving.

When someone does not offer you comfort and convenience,
It is a good opportunity for you to prove
Patience and tolerance.

When someone breaks an appointment,
It is a good opportunity to conquer
Anxiety and annoyance.

When someone leaves you,
It is a good opportunity to live
Peacefully.

When you do good deeds and others ignore them,
It is a good opportunity to overcome
Feeling badly
And to conquer the feeling of attachment.

When no one knows who you are,
It is a good opportunity for you

Varadhamma

Not to be.

When someone takes advantage of you,
It is a good opportunity to gain
A lesser ego.

**When someone intentionally offends you,
It is a good opportunity to forgive,
It expresses friendship toward them.
Do not be in a hurry for them
To apologize to you,
Otherwise they will still be heedless.
Wait for them, for the day of their repentance;
That will give them the opportunity to change.
That day is not too far away,
At least the second
Before their last breath.**

❋

Varadhamma

63. The Real Foolish Person
❊

Do not say that others don't know how to do some things;
They may be able to do other things better than you.

Do not say that others cannot think of some things,
They may be able to think of other things better than you.

Do not say others are foolish;
They may be smarter than you in other ways.

Do not say others are wrong;
They may be more right than you in other ways.

Do not say that others do not know;
They may know more than you in other subjects.

Do not say others do not have ability;
They may have more ability than you in other ways.

But of one who still creates suffering
Through violence to themselves and others
It should be said that:
That person cannot do anything,
Cannot think anything,
Is foolish, is wrong, does not know,
Does not have ability
In any aspects of life.

Varadhamma

64. Something Hard To Do

*

We can watch something all day long,
But to meditate on one peak for a time,
That is a hardship.

We can listen to something all day long,
But to listen to the heart beat once,
That is a hardship.

We can breathe in and out all day long,
But to be mindful of long breaths once before sleep,
That is a hardship.

We can say something all day long,
But to praise the triple gem in one word,
That is a hardship.

We can touch something all day long,
But to touch the withered flesh just once,
That is a hardship.

Varadhamma

We may be in a pleasant or unpleasant state all day long,
But to realize the whole process of
Suffering and no-suffering
Even once in our lives,
That is more hardship.

Varadhamma

65. The Righteousness

**Before going to bed, we should close the door tightly,
But open the window for ventilation.**

Open your hand for receiving
And hold it tightly, so it won't be lost.

When getting something from a shelf
Above a senior's head,
You should bow to say "Excuse me"
And then tiptoe to get it.

When you express your respect,
Sometimes you should stand up straight,
Sometimes you bow your body,
And sometimes you prostrate.

When speaking, you speak loudly with someone,
You speak softly with someone,
And keep silent with someone.

**When you give, you give much to someone,
You give moderately to someone,
You give little to someone,
And not give at all to someone.**

✻

Varadhamma

66. Don't Want To Be Neither Rich Nor Poor

✳

**Don't say you pity or feel an aversion to the poor.
The poor people have a duty
And responsibility as poor people,
Experiencing suffering in their way.
But your duty to them is
To comprehend the state of suffering
And the state of no-suffering.**

Don't praise or criticize the rich.
The rich have a duty and responsibility as the rich,
Experiencing suffering in their way.
But your duty to them is
To comprehend the state of suffering
And the state of no-suffering.

When the poor see poverty as suffering,
They will struggle to be free from being poor.
When the rich see wealth as suffering,
They will struggle to be free from being rich.

**Both rich and poor have the same destination
No suffering or *Nibbana.***

Varadhamma

People who say
They pity or feel an aversion to the poor,
Or praise or criticize the rich,
Do they really help anyone?
They themselves feel dissatisfied
And take part in creating the poor and the rich,
And by creating real antagonists in human society.

Varadhamma

67. No Hesitation

*

**Water never hesitates to flow
To the lower place.**

Fish never hesitate to struggle
To reach the pond.

Yellow leaves never hesitate
To fall from the branch.

Having seen the flame,
Insects never hesitate to swarm to it.

The evil person never hesitates to associate
With unwholesome things.

When you realize the harmfulness of suffering
With ultimate wisdom,
Your mind never hesitates to refrain from attachment.

**But when ignorance follows
The moment of contact and feeling,
It causes the mind to hesitate
In all phenomena.**

Varadhamma

68. Cause and Supporting Factors

✳

Human beings should not be extremely assertive,
Because that is not harmonious with the law of nature.

Do not say that a person is good or bad;
They may be good with someone but bad with someone,
Being good in this place
But bad in another place.
It depends on the person, time and space.

Don't say this person is extremely weak-minded
Or strong-minded;
They may be weak-minded with someone,
But strong-minded with someone else;
Being weak-minded at this moment,
But strong-minded at another moment;
Being weak-minded in this place,
But strong-minded at another place.
It depends on the person, time and space.

Don't say that this person has extremely
Good or bad behavior;
They may be well-behaved with someone
And not well-behaved with another;
Being well-behaved at this moment,
But not well-behaved at another moment;

Varadhamma

Being well-behaved in this place,
But not at another place.
It depends on the person, time and place.

Don't say this person is extremely
Solemn or merry.
They may be solemn with someone
But merry with another;
Being solemn at this moment,
But merry at another moment;
Being solemn in this place,
But merry at another place.
It depends on the person, time and space.

Having known this, one should not be extreme,
Going to one side or being surprised,
Interested, or shaken with phenomena,
But dwell in the ultimate truth.
That is: "It depends on cause and supporting factors."

What thing depends on cause and supporting factors?
That thing is suffering.
Do not depend on a person, time or space,
But depend on peace and harmony.
Then you will experience real happiness.

Varadhamma

69. Actual Thing

✳

We may say that water,
Except for giving coolness to others
In itself is cool as well.
Or water, because of its own coolness
Can give coolness to others.

We will say that from an external or internal place
It is equal.
But the real thing that certainly exists
Is genuinely cool water.

A Bodhisattva (Buddha to be)
Will first release all beings, such as
Hell beings, hungry ghosts, beasts,
Human beings, devas or Bhramins
From the one-minded world
To realize *Nibbana* and he will then attain *Nibbana.*

Or an Arahant (the noble person)
Who first practices for the realization of *Nibbana*
And later releases all beings, such as
Hell beings, hungry ghosts, beasts
Human beings, devas or Bhramins
From the one-minded world to *Nibbana.*

Varadhamma

We may say that from an external place
Or an internal place
It is equal.
But the real thing that certainly exists
Is to realize *Nibbana.*

We may say that
We help extinguish other peoples' suffering first
And help ourselves afterwards,
Or extinguish our own suffering first
And help others later,
Or help extinguish suffering in both
Ourselves and others together.

**The actual thing that truly exists
Is the mind which realizes
The "state of voidness":
That is the extinction of suffering
With nothing remaining in that moment.**

Varadhamma

70. Disliking

*

When you dislike cats,
The mice will surely tear your clothing.

When you dislike your neighbors,
The fence will be destroyed.

When you dislike salt,
You will eat bland foods.

When you dislike hard work,
You will not be able to work at any job.

When you dislike the wise,
You will associate with evil ones.

When you dislike the truth,
You will affiliate with deception.

When you dislike all things,
You dislike yourself the most.

Varadhamma

71. Sport Is Supreme Healing

The term sport means "Playing",
But not doing so frivolously, seduced by defilement,
Teasing, casual manners,
Committing vices, frivolous amusement,
Sensual entertainment, or tense competition.

All of these things make one anxious and un-relaxed.
But "playing" is relaxation,
Balancing body, mind and spirit.
It is not desire or attachment,
But is done with a void mind,
And its benefit is *Nirvana,*
The state of clear, calm and clean.

Do not say "We are going to play a sport"
Because the understanding becomes averted
To the misconception that "playing" for exercise
Requires specific equipment.
In reality, "play" and "sport" have the same meaning.

So what should be said is
"We sport." or "We do as sport",
Meaning that whatever we do,

Varadhamma

"Playing" or "relaxation",
Every gesture is without stress or tension
Or self indulgence.

"All work and no play makes Jack a dull boy."
Only work and no play makes Jack a dull boy.
This phrase has two concepts
Which are "work" and "play".
In different times and places
We separate work from play.
Jack works with stress and tension
With the desire for existence and non-existence
And expects relaxation by frivolous playing.

But be careful,
This combined with the desire for existence
And non-existence
Makes him more tired and anxious.
When leading a life with desire,
Jack never experiences the "true relaxation".
Life then is torment and suffering
In both physical and spiritual ways,
With unawareness of himself.

"All work with no play makes Jack a dull boy."
All work with lack of relaxation
Makes Jack a dull boy.

See! We do not separate work
And play, which is relaxation.
We relax with work and responsibility

Varadhamma

Or perform duty with relaxation;
We do work of all kinds with enjoyment.
Work is then efficient
And we have a clear, calm and cold mind
In the same duty, time and place;
It is not work with suffering.
Expecting happiness from frivolous playing
In reality creates more suffering.

Because of this misconception of "playing",
Desire and defilement have the opportunity to arise;
We then do not have full concentration in our work,
Only waiting for the work to be finished.
Later on we will enjoy defiled playing;
Working then becomes hellish
And full of torment and suffering.
Expecting heaven from defiled playing,
Both activities and behavior suffer.
We then never encounter
The middle way of life,
Which is the real peace.

We should say this concisely:
"Do work of all kinds with a mind that is void,"
Making mankind wise and perfect.

We used to say "What to do".
We never say "With what to do" or "How to do",
Saying only "do this" "do that".
But we never say "Do it with a relaxed mind".
We only observe the external duty,

Varadhamma

Never looking in our minds
Which control the working.
We are then foolish because
We cannot completely solve problems.

Religion teaches us to realize that
First, we have the outward duty that must be performed,
Second, the duty to prevent suffering from arising.
Everyone does the same thing:
For the external duty,
Let it be under the condition
Of cause and effect
Appropriate to each person.

We have no suffering, but void mind;
That is relaxation.
Playing in every kind of duty,
We are the wise person
And absolutely solve the problems.

Varadhamma

72. Nature

✳

You will not be surprised or marvel at the beehives.
If you stay and watch,
The bees are busy working all the time.

You will not doubt the ability of mountain climbers
If you participate in the same activity.

You will not see the cruelty of the war
If you were among the group who started it.

You will not see the courage of the warriors
Or their leaders,
If you are one of them.

You are not astonished at the
Genius of philosophers
If you study at the same academic level.

You will not see the mystery of space,
Of the sky or the depths of the ocean,
If you have explored them.

You do not see the mystery and profoundness

Varadhamma

Of Spirituality
If you practice insight meditation.

You do not see the supremacy of the noble persons
If you are cultivating wisdom from realization.

You will not see the greatness, mystery,
Or gravest of conditions in this world,
If you realize the true nature of all feelings,
Which are: impermanence and non-self.

73. No "I" in the World

✳

Even though this world is complicated in many ways,
If I were not born,
The complexity of the world
Would have no meaning for me
Because there is no I in this world.

Even though this world is complicated in many ways
And I have been born,
If I were not in that situation
I would not have contacted the complexity
Of the world by my sense organs.
The complexity of the world
Has no meaning for me,
Because this "world" lacks me.

Even though this world is complicated in many ways
And I have both been born
And am in the situation of
Having contacted the complexity
Of the world by my sense organs,
But I have no attachment to any objects,
The complexity of the world
Then has no meaning for me,
Because there is no "I" in this world.

✳

Varadhamma

About the Author ...

Venerable Varasak Varadhammo was born at Songkhla in the Southern part of Thailand on the 28th day of July, 1938. He went forth as a Buddhist Monk in July of 1968. From 1968 until 1991 Venerable Varadhammo studied and practiced *Buddhadhamma* and meditation with the *Most Venerable Buddhadāsa Indapañño Mahāthera* at *Suan Mokkhabalārāma, Chaiyā, Surat Thāni, Thailand.* Since late 1991 Venerable Varadhammo has resided at the Buddha-dharma Meditation Center in Hinsdale, Illinois. Venerable Varadhammo is a indefatigable *Dhamma Teacher* and writer having written and published more than forty books on Buddhism. His latest offering is entitled *"Suffering and No-Suffering"* which is now available at the Buddhadharma Meditation Center.

✳

BOOK RECOMMENED

BY
Sukhapabjai publishing

Keys to Natural Truth

By Buddhadasa Bhikkhu

Translated by Santikaro Bhikkhu

The keys in this book are intended to help open a clear and liveable path through our confusion and weakness into correct understanding of Dhamma (Natural Truth), so that the Dhamma in turn may illuminate life, reveal its secret, and quench all suffering (Dukkha).

There are five articles or "Keys" here.

The first, "Kalama Sutta, Help Us!" sets out a fundamental attitude of Buddhism. "Two Kinds of Language," the second key shows how to discriminate between the two levels of language which are intertwined in all spiritual speech and literature. And the third key, "Looking Within" shows us where to verify the truths taught by others. Both of these keys help us to apply the principle of the Kalama Sutta. "Happiness&Hunger," the fourth key is to clarify the proper motivation for Dhamma study and practice. The last key here, "The Dhamma - Truth of Samatha - Vipassana for the Nuclear Age," discusses a few important issues which are regularly confused.

Size : 13x18.4 cm
No. of pages : 232 P.

180.-

ANAPANASATI BHAVANA meditation

By Buddhadāsa Bhikkhu
Condensed by Chien Nurn Eng
Translated by James RatanaNantho Bhikkhu

This book aims at providing a guiding path leading to the proper practice of all the sixteen steps of Ānāpānasati in such a manner as to render it truly possible for anyone to adopt it as a handbook for self-help or do -it-yourself meditation practice, while at the same time conjuring a feeling in which one would feel as though one is receiving a face-to-face instruction from the meditation master himself, all of which will be of enornomous value to those who are interested in practicing Buddhist Dhamma.

Size : 13x18.4 cm No. of pages : 176 P. **150.-**

Buddhism In Thailand

Its Past and Its Present
By Dr.Karuna Kusalasaya

Buddhism in Thailand is a concise but authentic treatise on the spread of Budddhism to Thailand with its present situation in that country.

Buddhism is one of famous religions in the world. It has long history and fascinating teaching that many people found to be their answer of life. Buddhism doesn't exist only in Asia but it made a great headway in Europe and elsewhere. Thailand is perhaps the only country in the world where the king is constitutionally stipulated to be a Buddhist and the upholder of the Faith.

Size : 13x18.4 cm No. of pages : 100 P. **100.-**

The Buddha's Core Teachings

English - Thai Edition
By Suwat Chanchamnong

This bilingual text has been gleaned from Buddhist literatures, particularly those written by the highly respected Buddhist scholars, Phra Dhammapitaka (P.A. Payutto), Phra Dhepsophon [Prayoon Mererk] and Dr Sunthorn Plammintr. The English - Pali terms used in all parts of this English version are based on the Dictionary of Buddhism compiled by Phra Dhammapitaka. It is the writer's personal belief that this book is an invaluable reference for both students and the newcomers who are intersted in Buddhism.

Size : 14.5x21.0 cm No. of pages : 584 P.

250.-

Chaiya

Experience Exquisite
Insights of Thailand

More than a thousand years ago, this area blossomed as the Srivijaya Empire - a diverse Southeast Asian civilizaton, largely Buddhist and strongly in fluenced by India. Buddhism took root in this fabled "Golden Land" & from here spread to other Kingdoms - Nakorn Srithammraj, Lopburi, Sukhothai, Ayudhaya, & Ratanakosin (Bangkok & modern Thailand) - even as it slowly faded here. Today, only the ruins of ancient monuments & traces in the local culture remain: fables, children's lullabies, & Dhammic riddles in old manuscripts. Nonetheless, these prove that in the past the life & society of our ancestors were imbued with Buddha-Dhamma.

Size : 17.5x17.5 cm No. of pages : 180 P.

300.-

Things which we still pay too little interest to

By Buddhadāsa Bhikkhu

In three languages : Thai - English - Chinese

A conclusion of all that I have been talking about into something substantially short, just for the sake of your convenience here : The conclusive fact is that in the span of years that has slipped by, we have been paying too little attention to the 'Dhamma' which is the 'Heart' of our Buddhism.

We learn about 'Anattā' (impermanence), 'Suññata' (voidness), detachment and 'Paṭiccasamuppāda' (dependent origination) and the Four Noble Truths in the form of literature, philosophy and psychology, but not in the form of the actual practice that existed during the Buddha's time. We only talk about the way to implement and corelate our work in the proclaiming of our religion, but we forget to speak about the true Dhamma which ought to be proclaim far and beyond. We have been acting as though everyone of us has completed our job and all have become Arahants with nothing more to do with Dhamma. In actual facts, the things which we have proclaimed to the public is nothing but only matters of ethics or moral education for the society or politics. They are not 'Paramatadhamma' or Concepts of Ultimate Realities that constitute the main core of Buddhism.

Size : 14.5x21 cm

No. of pages : 84 P.

50.-